SUPER SMART INFORMATION STRATEGIES

YOUR FASCINATING FAMILY HISTORY

by Mary J. Johnson

CHERRY LAKE PUBLISHING • ANN ARBOR, MICHIGAN

A NOTE TO PARENTS AND TEACHERS: Please remind your children how to stay safe online before they do the activities in this book.

A NOTE TO KIDS: Always remember your safety comes first!

CHERRY LAKE Publishing

Published in the United States of America
by Cherry Lake Publishing
Ann Arbor, Michigan
www.cherrylakepublishing.com

Content Adviser: Gail Dickinson, PhD,
Associate Professor, Old Dominion University,
Norfolk, Virginia

Book design and illustration: The Design Lab

Photo credits: Cover, ©Lisa F. Young/Shutterstock, Inc.; page 4, ©iStockphoto.com/Blue_Cutler; page 15, ©iStockphoto.com/ArtisticCaptures; page 16, ©Konstantin Sutyagin/Shutterstock, Inc.; page 22, ©Gavril Bernad/Dreamstime.com; page 24, ©Ed Phillips/Shutterstock, Inc.; page 28, ©wavebreakmedia ltd/Shutterstock, Inc.

Library of Congress Cataloging-in-Publication Data
Johnson, Mary J., 1949–
Super smart information strategies: your fascinating family history/by Mary J. Johnson.
p. cm.—(Information explorer)
Includes bibliographical references and index.
ISBN-13: 978-1-61080-122-5 (lib. bdg.)
ISBN-13: 978-1-61080-268-0 (pbk.)
1. Genealogy—Juvenile literature. I. Title.
CS15.5.J64 2011
929'.1—dc22 2011000641

Cherry Lake Publishing would like to acknowledge the work of The Partnership for 21st Century Skills. Please visit *www.21stcenturyskills.org* for more information.

Printed in the United States of America
Corporate Graphics Inc.
July 2011
CLFA09

Table of Contents

CHAPTER ONE

What Is Genealogy?

Family history is often passed down by telling stories.

Do you like to listen to your parents, grandparents, aunts, or uncles tell stories about your family? Would you like to know more family stories? Do you like to tell stories yourself? One way to become your family's storyteller is to learn some of the techniques of genealogy—the study of ancestry and family history.

Every family has stories to tell. Your father might tell about his experiences as a soldier in a war zone. Your grandmother might tell about harvesting hay on the family farm. You might hear stories about family members who sailed on ships from Europe, Asia, or Africa. There could even be stories about family members born hundreds of years ago!

When you collect these stories, you are collecting oral history. They are the stories that are told and retold. They aren't always written down. This is where you come in. Like any good historian, you can collect these stories into a history—the history of your family! In this book, you will learn how to collect and organize your family stories and then share them.

Many teachers like to do "My Family History" projects. This book will help you do the best project possible. You can also put together your own family history project just for fun! The story you tell and the way you tell it will change, depending on what your family is like. The project doesn't even have to be about your own family. Professional genealogists research other people's families. You can look into the family histories of neighbors or friends. You just have to pick a place to start!

It is a good idea to start with some basics. The first person with a story to tell is YOU! You are the direct descendant of a father and mother and all the grandparents for generations before you. Start by gathering and writing down basic information about yourself. Then you can move on to your immediate family. Names, birth dates, and places of birth are all basic information. Gather that information for your immediate and extended family members. Then you can start to fill in the history that really defines your family.

TRY THIS!

Your first genealogy notes should include:

1. Your full name
2. The day, month, and year you were born
3. The exact name of the place you were born
4. The full names of all your brothers and sisters
5. The birth dates of all your brothers and sisters
6. The exact names of the places your brothers and sisters were born
7. Your parents' full names
8. The birth dates of your parents
9. The exact names of the places your parents were born
10. The date and place where your parents were married

Getting Started

Now you are ready to fill out an official family group sheet. Before you move to this step, take a look at these guidelines that can help you get started with genealogy:

- Write a man's name like this: JONES, Harold Edward
- Write a married woman's maiden name, the name she had before she was married, like this: CARNEY, Alice Ann
- Write dates like this: 8 Dec 1949 or 23 Apr 2001
- Fill out forms in pencil.
- When you do not know something, don't ever make it up!

As your project grows to include more generations of your family, you will fill out a family group sheet for each separate family—each father, mother, and their children.

DID YOU KNOW THIS?

You can find all kinds of genealogy forms online. The Web sites listed in the back of this book (see page 31) have links to forms such as the family group sheet.

CHAPTER TWO

Finding Evidence

Like a good detective, you will need to find evidence to prove that the information you write on genealogy charts is correct. So far, you have been able to fill in forms with names, dates, and places your family members know and remember. Genealogists always look for official papers and records to back up every bit of information—even their own birth dates!

Now is the time to start collecting official family papers, or documents. Ask your mother or father where to find vital records and other papers for your immediate family. Many of these have legal or sentimental importance. Families often store them in a safe place. Is your birth certificate in a baby book along with the date when your first tooth came in? Is there a file folder of immigration or military records in a desk drawer? Maybe a box of family papers is hiding in the corner of a closet. Be sure to ask before going through someone's things. Respecting a person's privacy is important!

Birth certificates provide basic information about family members.

TRY THIS!

Great information explorers know that it is important to make copies of family records. After all, you are making a keepsake for your family that may be passed on to the next generation. If you have a scanner or printer that makes copies, use it. You can also take photographs with a digital camera or cell phone and save them on a computer or print them. For now, make copies of:

- Birth certificates
- Marriage certificates
- Death certificates
- Adoption certificates

As you gather more genealogy "stuff," you will want to find a way to organize it. You can put everything in a loose-leaf binder with dividers. Begin each section with the family group sheet at the front of all the copies of records for that single family. You can also use colored file pockets to hold your growing collection.

Use a scanner to store images and documents on a computer.

Many genealogy projects include a family tree that you can display in a classroom or at home. A family tree is a chart in the form of a picture. It shows how family members are related by connecting them in certain ways. Brothers and sisters are connected to each other and to their parents. Their parents are connected to *their* brothers, sisters, and parents, and so on. The connections can go back for several generations.

When you make a family tree, have fun with it! You can make it any size you want. You can use any materials you like. It doesn't even have to look like a tree. Just remember to connect the family members in some way—with string, by placing parents above children by groups—to show how they are related to each other. Your family tree might include just your immediate family or all the cousins, aunts, uncles, and grandparents you know. It can even include your pets!

Try brainstorming family tree ideas with a friend or family member. Think about what shape you want your family tree to be and how family members will be connected. What pictures best represent your family? Has your family lived in the same area for a long time? Is there a family interest or hobby that has been passed down from generation to generation? The answers to these questions might give you a great idea!

Here are some creative family tree ideas:

- A fruit tree with family photos on apples, pears, or peaches
- A painted mural with your own paintings of family members
- A flower with family member names on petals
- A real tree with a hanging artifact to represent each family member
- A mobile made with wire coat hangers and yarn connecting parents to children and husbands to wives

A mobile family tree can hang from the ceiling.

When your project expands to the generation of your grandparents and great-grandparents, you can continue to fill out a family group sheet for each new family. In formal genealogy, however, you will use a pedigree chart when you begin to research further back in time. Pedigree refers to someone's direct ancestors. Ancestors are family members to whom a person is related directly, through parentage. For example, your parents, grandparents, and great-grandparents are part of your pedigree. Cousins, aunts, and uncles are not. A pedigree chart is a diagram that shows your pedigree. It includes your own direct ancestors, not your brothers, sisters, cousins, aunts, or uncles.

Most people begin with a standard pedigree chart that displays four or five generations. Some are fancy, some are plain. Choose the style that you like best!

You are "No. 1" on your pedigree chart. Your name goes on the first line. Follow this model: Paul Ramon LUCERO or Tanisha Ann WALKER. Include your birth date and place of birth.

Next, fill in the information about your father. His name goes on line 2. If you look to the right on the chart, you will notice that all the male lines have even numbers (except line 1 if you are a boy). Your father is 2, his father (your paternal grandfather) is 4, and so on. Do you see the pattern? Every father is double the number of his child—2, 4, 8, 16, 32, and so on for all generations.

Finish your father's lines with all the information that fits: his date of birth, marriage, and death. A complete chart also lists the places for each event.

Next, fill in the lines for your mother. What is her number? 3! Every female in your family will go into an uneven numbered blank on the chart: 3, 5, 7, 9, and so on. Be sure to use your mother's maiden name in capital letters. Add her date and place of birth.

A pedigree chart can look like this.

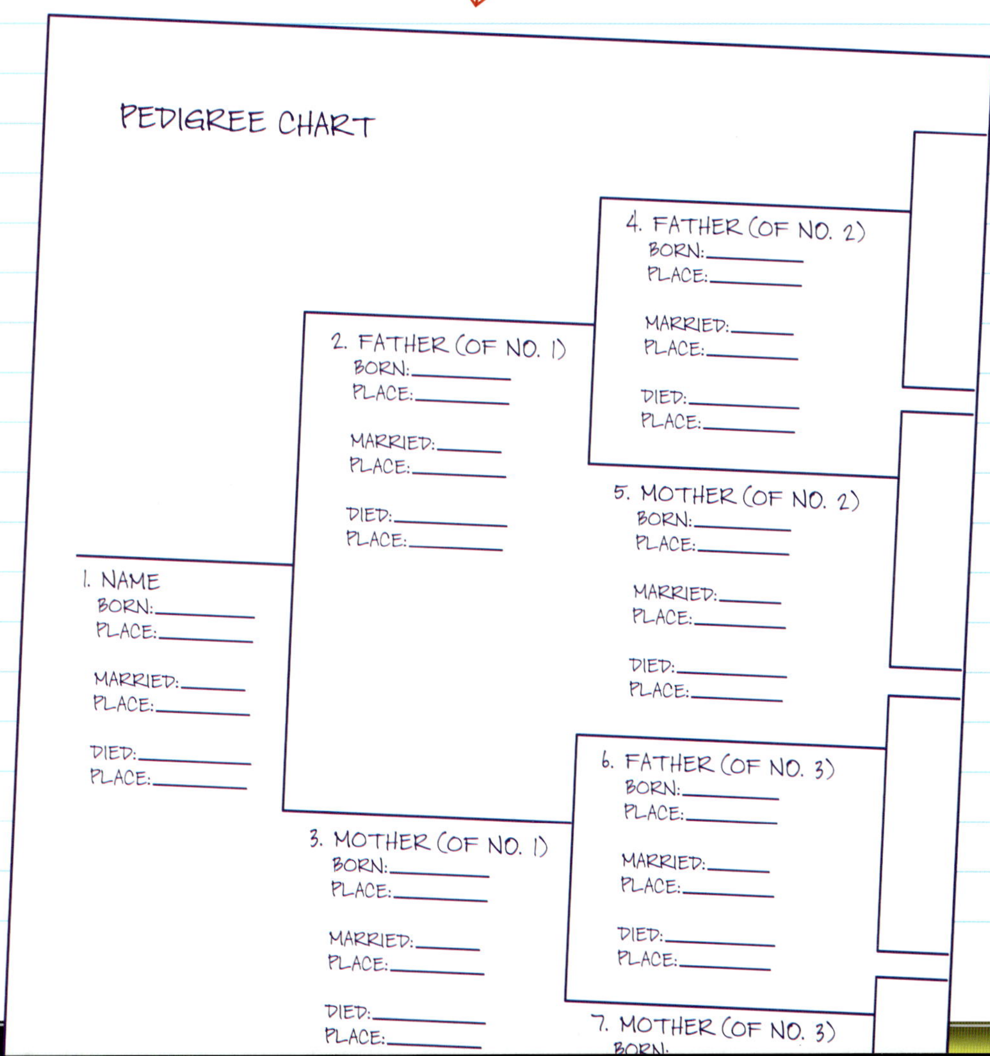

Now that you know the pattern, you can start filling in the next generation. As you move back in time, you will probably have to leave some lines blank. Don't worry! Every genealogist eventually runs into a dead end.

TRY THIS!

Putting together a family history can be challenging. Organization is important for all genealogists. It is also important to stick with the project and not give up! You can keep yourself organized and on task by trying a few tricks:

- Use your loose-leaf binder to keep each family group in order.
- Put the pedigree chart in the front of your binder and check it for missing information.
- Write evidence notes on the backs of your family group sheets.
- Keep a to-do list of detective ideas.

What if your family just doesn't fit the formal pedigree chart? You are not alone. Many people have stepparents. Some people live in blended families, with children of different parents. Maybe your parents are a same-sex couple. Maybe you are adopted. Nontraditional families may simply require nontraditional pedigree charts.

If you are adopted, you may decide to trace your adoptive parents and your birth family. If your stepfather raised you, you may want to put his ancestors on your pedigree chart. If you have stepbrothers or stepsisters, or adoptive brothers and sisters, try comparing your family histories. How are they different? How are they alike?

Everyone's family and family history is a little different.

Chapter Three: Oral History

CHAPTER THREE

Oral History

Family members sometimes remember different stories or details.

Now you have a basic description of family members and how they are related. It is time to start making your family history come alive. Which family member might help you fill in the details and bring your ancestors' stories to life? Chances are you have already asked your mother or father for some help. Older relatives—grandparents, great-grandparents, great-aunts, and great-uncles—have lived longer. They have stored away years of memories. Now is the time to talk to them.

When you interview a relative and write or record your interview, you are collecting oral history. You are adding real voices to your family's story. With preparation and practice, you can become a fine oral historian for your family. For your first oral history interview, choose a family member who makes you feel comfortable. For example, you might want to ask a kind, encouraging grandmother or a favorite uncle.

Many skills go into a successful oral history interview. Some people do not like to talk about themselves. Others do not think they have anything important to say. Some might even have painful memories. Be sure to ask politely for the interview. Tell your interviewee that you want to honor the family by listening to and recording some of the family stories.

You can also suggest that your interviewee gather a few photographs and other keepsakes. Then you can talk about them together. This can help put you both at ease.

A keepsake can help bring family history alive.

TRY THIS!

Write down some questions that you would like to ask. Keep in mind that your questions will only guide the interview. Your conversation won't run smoothly if you just go through a checklist. Be curious, not bossy!

An interview shouldn't last more than 1 hour. Usually, one memory leads to another, but you will want to write down your questions anyway. Here are some categories to use when you write your questions:

- Growing up
- School and friends
- Brothers, sisters, parents
- Holidays
- Work
- Favorite things
- Home
- Military service
- Dating, marriage, children
- Travel

Can you think of other categories? What information about your ancestors do you think your interviewee can tell you? Now is your chance to fill in the gaps.

Always write down your name and the name of the person you are interviewing before you begin an interview. You should also write down the date and the location of the interview.

You might be a little nervous during your first oral history interview, but don't worry. As long as you remember to listen, you will do a great job. That's because nobody can become a great interviewer without first being an excellent listener. Be sure not only to listen, but also to show that you're interested in what the person is saying. If the interviewee tells a funny story, feel free to laugh! If the story is sad or scary, don't be afraid to react. By showing that you are involved in what someone is saying, you will encourage the person to talk.

You have written a list of questions, but how can you use your listening skills to make the conversation feel natural? Three magic questions will help you:

- Why?
- What did you think about that?
- What happened to you?

Sometimes the best skill of all is silence. We all need time to think!

Take notes during your interview to help you remember what you heard.

It's a great idea to record your oral history interview. You can capture the voice of your relative with a small digital recorder and save it to a computer. With a video camera, you can record the voice and the moving image. Both let you go back and listen again. The recordings become a part of your family keepsakes, too.

Your school or library might have a recorder you can use. If someone in your family has a smartphone, such as an iPhone, you can use that. If you use a video camera, always try to set it up on a tripod. The quality will be better, and you will be free to ask questions and pay attention to the interview.

Chapter Three: Oral History

DID YOU KNOW THIS?

Do your grandparents live too far away to interview in person? If you both have computers, you can use software such as Skype. Skype lets you make free calls over the Internet. If both computers have cameras, you can even see each other when you talk! Extra software called a plug-in can be used to record your Skype interview, including video. You can ask a librarian, teacher, or parent to help you set up Skype.

Your computer can help you interview someone who lives far away.

Remember to send a note thanking your interviewee.

Always write a thank-you note after you interview someone. Do this first and then get to work on the recording. Listen to or watch your recording again. Write down any new information on your family group sheets or your pedigree chart. Most oral historians also transcribe their interviews. This means that they go through the recording line by line and write down what was said. You may need some help with this big job. The transcribed interview, or transcription, serves as a good reference if you want to check a fact or quote the interviewee. Accuracy is always important in any research project. A transcription can help keep your research accurate and thorough.

THINK ABOUT THIS!

What have you learned from your first oral history interview? Think about which questions worked well. How can you improve the questions that did not work as well? Did you listen carefully? If you recorded your interview, how could the picture and sound quality be improved? What will you do differently the next time? Can you think of any new questions to ask?

CHAPTER FOUR

Digging Deeper

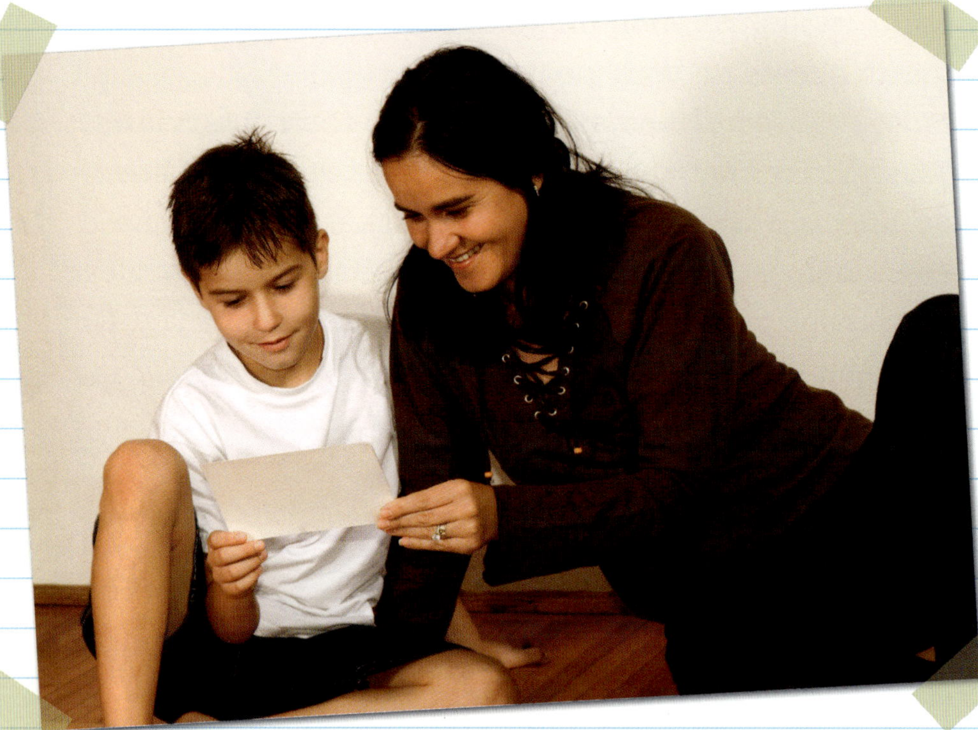

You might be able to collect old photographs during your interviews.

When you filled out your family group sheet, you collected a few records and documents such as birth and marriage certificates. Maybe the family member you interviewed brought along some old photographs, birth certificates, or school papers.

Don't stop there! Think of other evidence that might be hiding somewhere. Has anyone kept old letters? Did an ancestor write a diary? Is there a family Bible? Can you find farm records, club records, or estate sale ads? You can add every artifact ever left by an ancestor to your research. Be sure to keep track of these artifacts. You don't want to lose or damage them.

Today, genealogists look for many records on the Internet. Groups all over the world are putting lists of records on public Web sites. Professional genealogists follow and learn from one another on Twitter and Facebook. The Internet makes this an exciting time to be a genealogist!

If you know some basic information about an ancestor (full name, birth date, and death date), you can begin to search online for many types of records:

- Church, synagogue, or mosque records
- Immigration records
- Cemetery records
- Census records
- Obituaries (sometimes called death notices)
- City and telephone directories
- Military and veterans' records
- Land records
- Court records and wills

The Web sites listed on page 31 have links to all sorts of online records.

Veterans may have medals and other artifacts to show you.

You can write to the National Archives for information if one of your ancestors served in the military. Ask an adult for help with the forms and information needed to make a request. The National Archives will want a lot of details from you.

You might want to interview a veteran from your family. The Veterans History Project at the Library of Congress has a field kit to help you interview people who have served in the military. The kit includes advice for doing an interview and a wonderful list of questions to ask. Your teacher can even use the Veterans History Project materials for a class project. The advice in this kit is important. Some veterans do not want to talk about their experiences. Keep this in mind when you ask for an interview.

If you are really lucky, you may find a news item about an ancestor in an old newspaper. Libraries and museums are putting thousands of pages from historic newspapers online. If you have a computer, a good place to start is a national program called Chronicling America. You can also call your public library to ask if it has local newspapers online.

DID YOU KNOW THIS?

Old newspapers used old-fashioned words and forms of names. When you search for ancestors' names, try to think of how they wrote and spelled them back then.

- Use the husband's name for married women: Mrs. Arnold Payton or Mrs. Harold Keller.
- Use short forms of common first names: Th. for Thomas, Chas. for Charles, Wm. for William.

If you know the name of a business where an ancestor worked, try looking for advertisements by that name. What you find might surprise you!

CHAPTER FIVE

Sharing Your Family's Story

You're near the end of your first genealogy research project. Now is the time to think of ways to share what you have found. With a little extra effort, you can make a gift that someone in your family will treasure for a long time.

You have been collecting bits and pieces of family stories. Maybe you will want to share the story of one photograph or one family artifact. Maybe you will want to put a whole collection together. There are many ways to tell your family story!

Now you can share what you found with your family!

TRY THIS!

Can you think of a special person who would love to receive a family memory gift from you?

- Put together a collage of copies of family photographs.
- Build a diorama of an ancestor's house.
- Draw a map of the places your ancestors lived. Mark each place with a pin or a picture.
- Write the story of a family artifact.
- Make a scrapbook of all your family history discoveries.
- Put together a book of family recipes.

You can also share genealogy time with a special family member. One idea is to visit a cemetery where one of your ancestors is buried. Take a photograph of the headstone or try doing a rubbing of the information on the tombstone.

A diorama can show what an ancestor's house looked like.

Family stories can be shared by creating a digital story on a computer. A digital story is a short movie, about 2 or 3 minutes long. You put it together with photographs of family members, scanned family papers, and photographs of objects that mean something to your family. It's a good idea to use no more than 15 items! You add your voice to tell the story, and you can also put in videos and music.

You don't need fancy equipment to put together a digital story, but you may want to ask your school

A digital story can be shared with any family member who has a computer.

You can combine pictures, video, and sound in one presentation.

librarian or teacher for help with the software. You can use iMovie on a Mac or Movie Maker on a Windows computer. You can also search for free Web sites made for digital storytelling.

What story do you want to tell? That is the most important part of all! No matter what kind of digital story you choose to tell, try to keep it simple. Just like the oral history project, you need to plan it and practice it. The story is more important than the special effects. You don't have to be a professional movie producer to save memories!

Every family is special, and every family has stories to tell and share. Make genealogy your hobby, and you can become your family's storyteller. There are dozens of ways to share your discoveries. Members of your family may discover something they hadn't known before!

Glossary

ancestors **(AN-ses-turz)** members of your family who lived a long time ago, usually before your grandparents

archives **(AHR-kivz)** places where documents, letters, diaries, photos, and other information are stored

artifact **(AHR-tuh-fact)** an object of history made by a human

diorama **(dye-uh-RA-muh)** a three-dimensional model

estate sale **(i-STATE SALE)** a sale of the property and other things that a person leaves behind when he or she dies

family group sheet **(FAM-uh-lee GROOP SHEET)** a paper listing the father, mother, and each child of a family

interviewee **(in-tur-vyoo-EE)** a person who is interviewed

maiden name **(MAY-duhn NAYM)** a woman's last name before marriage

oral history **(OR-uhl HIS-tur-ee)** stores about the past that have been told and retold but not written down paternal

pedigree chart **(PED-i-gree CHAHRT)** a chart showing a person's direct ancestors

rubbing **(RUHB-ing)** a picture made by coloring on paper over a textured surface, such as the words on a gravestone

transcribe **(tran-SCRIBE)** write down the contents of a tape recording word for word

vital records **(VYE-tuhl REK-urdz)** government documents noting birth, death, marriage, and divorce information

Find Out More

BOOKS

Beller, Susan Provost. *Roots for Kids*. Baltimore: Genealogical Publishing, 2007.

Ollhoff, Jim. *Beginning Genealogy*. Edina, MN: ABDO Publishing, 2010.

WEB SITES

Cyndi's List

www.cyndislist.com/kids.htm

Visit the Kids and Teens page at this gateway to genealogy sites.

FamilySearch

www.familysearch.org/

Search for family group sheets and pedigree charts at the Learn tab.

National Archives

www.archives.gov/research/genealogy/

Explore the National Archives site to learn more about geneaology.

RootsWeb

www.rootsweb.ancestry.com/

Explore what's available on the free part of Ancestry.com.

Index

About the Author

Mary J. Johnson is a former Colorado school librarian. She loves reading, technology, travel, foreign languages, and hiking. She writes "The Primary Source Librarian" blog. This is her first book for kids.